Young Naturalist
Field Guides

Rabbits, Squirrels, and Chipmunks

by Mel Boring

illustrations by Linda Garrow

Gareth Stevens Publishing
MILWAUKEE

DEDICATION

To my mother, Helen Tuthill, who first taught me love,
and taught me to love all living creatures.

ACKNOWLEDGMENTS

Librarians help make books, and this book was no exception. My special thanks to
Bob Lane of the University of Iowa Biology Library for his help.

**For a free color catalog describing Gareth Stevens Publishing's list of high-quality
books and multimedia programs, call 1-800-542-2595 (USA) or
1-800-461-9120 (Canada). Gareth Stevens Publishing's Fax: (414) 225-0377.**

Library of Congress Cataloging-in-Publication Data

Boring, Mel, 1939-
   Rabbits, squirrels, and chipmunks/by Mel Boring; illustrated by
Linda Garrow.
     p. cm. -- (Young naturalist field guides)
   Originally published: Minocqua, Wis.: NorthWord Press, 1996, in series:
Take along guide.
   Includes bibliographical references and index.
   Summary: Describes the physical characteristics, habitat, and diet of
twenty-eight kinds of rabbits, squirrels, and chipmunks.
   ISBN 0-8368-2146-7 (lib. bdg.)
   1. Rabbits--Juvenile literature.   2. Squirrels--Juvenile literature.
3. Chipmunks--Juvenile literature. [1. Rabbits.   2. Squirrels.
3. Chipmunks.] I. Garrow, Linda, ill. II. Title. III. Series.
QL737.L32B66   1998
599.36--dc21   97-51325

This North American edition first published in 2000 by
Gareth Stevens Publishing
1555 North RiverCenter Drive, Suite 201
Milwaukee, Wisconsin 53212 USA

Based on the book, *Rabbits, Squirrels and Chipmunks*, written by Mel Boring, first
published in the United States in 1996 by NorthWord Press, Inc., Minocqua, Wisconsin.
© 1996 by Mel Boring. Illustrations by Linda Garrow. Book design by Lisa Moore.
Additional end matter © 2000 by Gareth Stevens, Inc.

Printed in Mexico

1 2 3 4 5 6 7 8 9 04 03 02 01 00

CONTENTS

Rabbits, Squirrels and Chipmunks

Metric Conversion Table

1 foot = 0.3048 meter
1 inch = 2.54 centimeters
1 mile = 1.609 kilometers
1 ounce = 28.33 grams
1 pound = 0.4536 kilogram
1 yard = 0.9144 meter

RABBITS

Rabbits are common sights in the countryside and even in the city. They are famous for their fluffy tails and big ears. Their tails are about 2 inches long and look like puff-balls. Their ears can swing in any direction to pick up the slightest sounds.

Many people think a rabbit's eyes are sharp, because they eat carrots. But rabbit eyesight is not as sharp as their hearing. Their eyes are on the sides of their heads, however, so they can see all around.

Rabbit noses help them sniff out danger. A rabbit's whiskers are long but usually light colored, so they are not very easy to see. A rabbit's back legs are longer and stronger than the front legs. Many rabbits thump their hind feet on the ground as a danger alarm.

Some rabbits are hares. What many people call the snowshoe "rabbit" is really the snowshoe hare. Jackrabbits are hares, too. Hares are bigger but skinnier than most rabbits. And hares are faster.

Most rabbits and hares do not dig burrows for homes. They scratch a shallow "bowl" out of the ground, called a form. Forms are usually hidden under bushes and trees. Rabbits spend the daytime there, going out to eat from evening to morning.

Have fun hopping into the world of rabbits!

EASTERN COTTONTAIL

WHAT IT EATS

Eastern cottontails eat a lot of different things. They eat weeds and almost every kind of berry and fruit. When they can get into a garden they will eat the lettuce, cabbage, beans and carrots they find. But they will not dig them up.

In the winter, their favorite food is sumac. Sumac is high in fat, so it gives them body heat in cold weather.

WHAT IT LOOKS LIKE

The tail of this rabbit looks like a fluffy ball of cotton bouncing away from you. Usually the eastern cottontail hops along slowly. It also sits up on its hind legs often, to get a better view of its surroundings.

An eastern cottontail is grayish brown on top, flecked with black. It has a reddish patch on the back of its neck. Underneath, it is creamy white. The underside of its tail is pure white. That is why it is called a "cottontail." This rabbit often has a white spot on its forehead.

Eastern cottontails are 14 to 18 inches long, and weigh 2 to 4 pounds.

INTERESTING FACTS

Eastern cottontails can run as fast as 20 miles per hour.

WHERE TO FIND IT

Eastern cottontails live in brushy places, fields, woods and farmlands.

They can be found all over the eastern half of the United States, except New England. These cottontails also live from the Dakotas to Texas, New Mexico and Arizona.

SWAMP RABBIT

WHAT IT LOOKS LIKE

The swamp rabbit is a swimming rabbit. All rabbits can swim if they have to, but this one travels by water most of the time. To escape enemies, it ducks underwater with only its nose showing. Swamp rabbits have extra skin between their toes that helps them swim. Their big feet with spreading toes also help them walk through mud.

The swamp rabbit can be over 21 inches long. It weighs up to 6 pounds. Its fur is rough, and brown-gray with black patches. It is white underneath, with a very short, thin tail. It has reddish feet.

WHAT IT EATS

The swamp rabbit is called the "cane-cutter rabbit" in the South, because its favorite food is cane, a tall grass that grows there. It also eats sedge plant, as well as herbs that grow in water. It likes corn, too.

WHERE TO FIND IT

These rabbits live in swampy, marshy places along rivers and streams. They can be found from Georgia to eastern Texas, and from southern Indiana and Illinois along the Ohio and Mississippi rivers to the Gulf of Mexico.

MARSH RABBIT

The marsh rabbit is a good swimmer, but it is even better at floating. In Georgia, its nickname is "pontoons" because it floats like a boat.

WHAT IT EATS

The marsh rabbit nibbles at reeds, and digs up wild potatoes and amaryllis bulbs. It also eats cane grass. In winter it eats tree leaves and twigs.

WHAT IT LOOKS LIKE

Marsh rabbits are slow runners. Walking or running, they put down one paw at a time like a cat or dog. But they can also hop and swim. A marsh rabbit gets away from its enemies by floating motionless among water plants, with its ears tucked down and just its nose and face above the water.

Marsh rabbits can also walk on just their hind legs. Most rabbits cannot do this, but the marsh rabbit does it often.

Marsh rabbits are dark red-brown, with lighter-brown tummies. They weigh about 3 1/2 pounds. Their small ears are about 2 inches long, and their tails are only about 1 1/2 inches long. The tail is brown underneath.

WHERE TO FIND IT

Marsh rabbits rest in brush, or in hollow logs and stumps. But they most often take shelter among tall grass and cattails in swamps.

This rabbit lives in the South, from Virginia through Florida and up to Alabama.

7

BRUSH RABBIT

WHAT IT LOOKS LIKE

The brush rabbit is a small, dark rabbit. It grows from 11 to 15 inches long and weighs about 1 or 2 pounds. Brush rabbits are gray-brown to brown, and speckled with black. Its tail is often shorter than 1 inch long, so you seldom see it.

"Brush" is part of the brush rabbit's name because it never hops farther than a few feet from thick, dense brush. It has shorter ears and legs than most rabbits. So it cannot hear enemies sneaking up as well and cannot run away as fast.

WHAT IT EATS

These rabbits feed mostly at night and eat herbs and grasses. One sign of brush rabbits is grass chewed down very short. Green clover is also one of their favorite meals. They eat plantain and berries, and twigs, bark and buds of Douglas fir trees in winter.

WHERE TO FIND IT

Brush rabbits do not dig burrows and rarely use the homes of other animals. Instead, brush rabbits tunnel into the dense brush.

Brush rabbits are found from Oregon's Columbia River to Baja California. They live along the western slopes of mountain ranges. They also live in cities and towns, feeding on lawns.

PYGMY RABBIT

WHAT IT EATS

Sagebrush is the pygmy rabbit's favorite food. It does not really eat much else. Sometimes it will eat a little rabbit brush.

WHAT IT LOOKS LIKE

The pygmy rabbit is the smallest rabbit of all. Less than 1 foot long, its ears are only about 2 inches long. The ears are covered with fine, silky hairs.

Their fur is peppery-brown, with light brown on their chests and legs. They have a white spot on each side of their noses. Pygmy rabbits weigh about 1 pound. Their tails are gray on top and bottom, and very short.

Unlike most other rabbits, pygmy rabbits are very social. They often live together in groups.

INTERESTING FACTS

Pygmy rabbits move close to the ground and do not hop as high as other rabbits.

WHERE TO FIND IT

The pygmy digs burrows, usually on slopes in soft, moist soil. Their burrows and tunnels go a little deeper than one yard beneath the sage and rabbit brush. Look for their small burrow doors. They are about 3 inches wide.

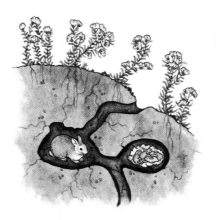

You will find pygmy rabbits in the western United States, in Montana, Idaho, Washington, Oregon, California, Nevada and Utah.

9

EUROPEAN RABBIT

WHAT IT EATS

When very hungry, the European rabbit will eat almost any green plant. It likes short grasses, herbs and leafy plants best.

WHERE TO FIND IT

European rabbits dig burrows. They are only active at night.

European rabbits live in brushy places and open fields. In the past 100 years, they have been brought from Europe to the United States on the west and east coasts. Today, they can be found in many parts of the U.S.

WHAT IT LOOKS LIKE

The European rabbit is the most common rabbit in the world.

It is rusty brown, with white on its tummy and inside its ears. It has a creamy patch on the back of its neck. Underneath, this rabbit's tail is white. It grows 18 to 24 inches long, and weighs 3 to 5 pounds.

European rabbits are social rabbits. Some live together in large groups of over 400 rabbits! These groups have a "king" rabbit and a "queen" rabbit.

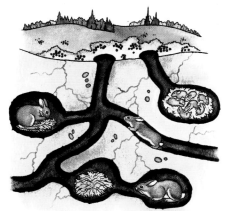

BLACK-TAILED JACKRABBIT

WHAT IT LOOKS LIKE

Although the black-tail is called "rabbit," it is really a hare. It is the best known and most common hare.

Black-tailed jackrabbits have very long ears, up to 6 inches long! These large rabbits can grow to be 2 feet long. They weigh as much as 8 pounds.

Sometimes black-tailed jackrabbits walk on all fours like a dog, instead of hopping. They have long legs and long, thick fur. Their fur is brown-gray with cream, and peppered with black. Underneath, they are white. Black-tails are the only hares with black on the top of their tails. The tips of their ears are also black.

WHAT IT EATS

Black-tailed jackrabbits eat at night and rest during the day. They eat sage-brush, rabbit brush and prickly-pear cactus. They also eat mesquite, snake-weed, grama grass, greasewood, alfalfa and saltbrush. Sometimes they eat voles.

WHERE TO FIND IT

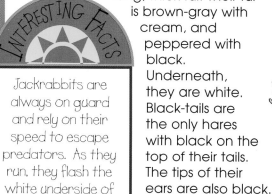

The black-tailed jackrabbit lives from South Dakota to Washington, and from there south to Mexico. It is usually the one you see along western highways, especially at night, eating the grasses that grow by the roadside.

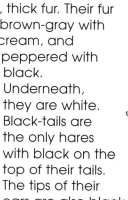

INTERESTING FACTS

Jackrabbits are always on guard and rely on their speed to escape predators. As they run, they flash the white underside of their tails to warn other rabbits.

WHITE-TAILED JACKRABBIT

WHAT IT EATS

White-tailed jackrabbits eat all kinds of plants, such as clover, alfalfa, filaree, spiderling, and prickly pear cactus. In winter, they eat twigs, buds, bark, and dried plants.

WHAT IT LOOKS LIKE

White-tailed jackrabbits wear two coats of fur, one in summer and the other in winter. During the summer, they are gray-brown. Before winter, they shed and put on a new gray or white coat. They have gray-white underparts.

The white-tailed jackrabbit's ears have black edges, which turn mostly white in winter. It has a white tail all year long.

These rabbits weigh from 5 to 9 pounds. They can grow to be 2 feet long.

This rabbit jumps over anything it has to. It could easily leap over your head! Like most hares, when the white-tailed jackrabbit is chased, it jumps straight up every few leaps to make a "spy hop" on its enemy.

WHERE TO FIND IT

These rabbits sprint around the West, from Montana to New Mexico. They can also be found from central California to Lake Michigan. They live in grassland plains and sagebrush desert.

SNOWSHOE HARE

WHAT IT EATS

Snowshoe hares eat mainly at night. They hide during the day beneath trees and come out in late afternoon. The snowshoe dines on the bark and tender tips of aspen, pine, spruce, white birch and white cedar trees. In summer, they munch grasses, clover, lupines, dandelions and strawberries.

WHAT IT LOOKS LIKE

The snowshoe hare's big feet keep it from getting stuck in the snow. When other animals bog down in snowdrifts, the snowshoe hare goes dashing through the forest. It has extra hair on its feet that keeps it from sinking, like using "snowshoes."

A snowshoe hare's fur changes color from dark brown in summer to white in winter. The tips of its ears are black in winter. Between summer and winter its fur is brown and white.

The snowshoe hare is larger than most rabbits. It weighs from 2 to 5 pounds, and grows up to 21 inches long.

INTERESTING FACTS

Even if the temperature stayed warm and there was no snow on the ground, a snowshoe hare's fur would still turn white in winter.

WHERE TO FIND IT

Snowshoes can be found across the northern United States and in the Pacific Coast and Rocky Mountain forests, as far south as New Mexico. They can also be found in Appalachian pine forests south to Tennessee.

CAPE HARE

INTERESTING FACTS

The cape hare gives a warning noise to enemies by grating its teeth. Other hares nearby will also make the teeth-grating sound.

WHAT IT LOOKS LIKE

Cape hares are large and lanky. Some weigh over 13 pounds and grow almost 28 inches long. They have kinky fur that is brown, streaked with black. They are white beneath, with black tail-tops and black-tipped ears. In the winter, their fur is more gray than brown.

The cape hare has lots of escape tricks. It will double back on enemies chasing it and slip in behind them. It can easily leap over a 5-foot wall. It has been known to lead enemies onto ice thick enough to hold itself, but too thin for the enemies. It can even swim across wide rivers.

WHERE TO FIND IT

The cape hare can be found in New York, Vermont, New Hampshire, Massachusetts, Connecticut, Pennsylvania, New Jersey and Maryland. It is in Michigan, Wisconsin and Minnesota, too.

WHAT IT EATS

The cape hare eats grasses, herbs and fruits in summer, and switches to buds, twigs and bark in winter. Some of its summer favorites are clover, wheat, corn, berries and apples. In winter it eats the bark of apple, peach and cherry trees.

MAKE A RABBIT PAPERWEIGHT

You can make a Pygmy Rabbit or a Snowshoe Hare—or any rabbit you like—for your very own. It can be a paperweight for your desk or a decoration for your room. You can tell the sizes of the ears and the feet from the drawings in this book.

WHAT YOU NEED

- modeling clay
- pen or pencil
- stiff paper or cardboard
- scissors
- Popsicle stick
- 2 pipecleaners
- 1 cottonball
- glue

WHAT TO DO

1 Shape the clay into three balls: a large one for the body, a small one for the head, and a tiny one for the nose. (Also make pieces for the feet if you want.)

2 Press the head onto the body.

3 Press the nose onto the head.

4 Draw two ears on the paper or cardboard. Cut them out. Stick them into the top of the head.

5 Draw lines for the eyes and mouth with the Popsicle stick.

6 Cut the pipecleaners into four pieces for the whiskers. Poke them in around the nose.

7 Let your rabbit harden overnight.

8 Glue the cottonball to the body for a tail.

After the rabbit hardens, you can paint it. If you make a large enough rabbit, you can put it outside to invite other rabbits to visit.

BUILD A RABBIT REFUGE

A tangled pile of brush means rabbits can find shelter and escape enemies.
You can build a rabbit refuge that will keep them safe and give you the
chance to see them up close. And by giving the rabbits something good to
munch on, you can be sure they will keep coming back.

WHAT YOU NEED

▼

- small branches and twigs (that are less than 2 inches thick and 10 feet long), tree and hedge clippings

- *Rabbit munchies:*
  - clover
  - dandelions
  - carrots
  - carrot tops
  - celery
  - celery tops
  - lettuce
  - radishes
  - grass clippings

WHAT TO DO

▼

1 Pick a place where rabbits will feel safe, where there is not too much activity or noise. It should be about 10 feet wide and 10 feet long. A smaller space may also work.

2 Put the longest branches in the middle of the spot, tangling them up as much as you can. Rabbits do not like neat, tidy places, so make the branches all jumbled in a pile that fills up your space. The pile should be at least 3 feet high.

3 Poke the smaller branches and twigs into the jumbled jungle. Push enough of them in so that you cannot see the ground below the refuge. Do not be worried that rabbits will not be able to get in. They can squeeze through tiny openings, and they will want all the privacy they can get.

4 Place a few small piles of the munchies around the edges of the Rabbit Refuge. It is better not to overload them, or try to put them inside the refuge. If your piles are too deep, the food may spoil and mold at the bottom. So make your piles no deeper than about two handfuls in each spot.

Now stay away from the Rabbit Refuge, and look out through your window from time to time. If there are rabbits in your neighborhood, they will come. The best times to see them are early in the morning and near dusk. Watch for them from a safe distance at first. Later, they may feel safe enough for you to get closer to them.

SQUIRRELS

Not all squirrels are tree squirrels. Some are ground squirrels that do not climb trees. They have shorter, skinnier tails, and "talk" a lot more than tree squirrels. There is hardly a ground squirrel without a whistle, a squeak or a buzz.

Squirrels are famous for their bushy tails, and those tails come in handy. In the rain it is a squirrel's "umbrella." When it is cold, their tails are used like blankets. If they fall from a tree, their tails parachute them to a soft landing.

Ground squirrels fill their burrows with nuts and seeds for mid-winter snacks. Tree squirrels also eat nuts and seeds, but they bury them in the ground. Sometimes they forget where some nuts are buried and new trees grow.

Most squirrels are active during the day. So you might see more squirrels than any other wild animal. Wherever squirrels eat, they leave behind "crumbs" from their nutty feasts. So watch for them hopping, skipping, leaping and even flying!

GRAY SQUIRREL

WHAT IT LOOKS LIKE

A gray squirrel's coat looks like it has been salted and peppered. Some black hairs and some white hairs make the whole coat look gray. The gray squirrel is bright white underneath, with tan on its ears and face. You can be sure that it is a gray squirrel if it has white-tipped hairs around its bushy tail.

This squirrel is 18 to 20 inches long including its tail. It weighs about 1 pound.

A gray squirrel can run on the ground more than 12 miles per hour, and up or down a tree almost as fast!

WHAT IT EATS

Hickory nuts, beech-nuts, walnuts and acorns are on the gray squirrel's menu. So are seeds, corn, fruits, berries, flowers, mushrooms and caterpillars. Its favorite spring treat is sweet icicles of sap from frozen maple trees.

WHERE TO FIND IT

The gray squirrel's den is usually in a hollow part of a tree about 40 feet off the ground. They also build twiggy leaf nests, usually near their dens. They prefer shadier wooded areas. You will find lots of little holes in the ground around this squirrel's home, because they bury every nut they find in a separate hole.

Gray squirrels are found nearly everywhere in the eastern half of the United States. You will find them in woodlands, suburbs and city parks, wherever large shade trees have food and hollows for dens.

Interesting Facts

A gray squirrel's top front teeth grow about 6 inches a year, so it has to chew to keep them worn down.

19

FOX SQUIRREL

You can tell which nuts have been eaten by fox squirrels. They tear the shells to pieces. Other squirrels gnaw a hole in one or both ends of the shell to get the nut out.

WHAT IT EATS

Acorns are a fox squirrel's favorite food. They also like hickory, beech, hazel and butternuts. Fruits and berries are food for them. And they love corn on the cob. They even eat cherry seeds, plum stones and thornapple pits.

WHAT IT LOOKS LIKE

In the North, the fox squirrel is the color of the red fox. That is how it got its name. It also has a bushy tail like a fox. This squirrel is the largest of all tree squirrels. It grows 18 to 29 inches long and weighs from 1 to 3 pounds.

In some states fox squirrels are as gray as gray squirrels. In the South, this squirrel is black and often has a white nose and tail-tip. You can tell a fox squirrel by its large size. It also has yellowish tips on its tail hairs.

WHERE TO FIND IT

Fox squirrels prefer a hollow in an oak or hickory tree to live in. You will find fox squirrels in the eastern half of the United States, except in New England. Some fox squirrels live in the West Coast states, from Washington to California.

In the South, they live in cypress and mangrove swamps, and places with pine trees.

RED SQUIRREL

WHAT IT LOOKS LIKE

This little squirrel has a loud voice. It looks like it is dressed in a rusty red coat and gray-white vest. During the summer, a black side stripe separates the red from the white. Its tail matches its coat, with a wide black border frosted with white. The red squirrel has a white eye ring that stands out brightly.

Red squirrels are less than 16 inches long, nose to tail-tip, and weigh about 1/2 pound.

WHAT IT EATS

Red squirrels eat seeds from tulip, sycamore, maple and elm trees, plus hickory nuts and acorns. They are also very fond of mushrooms. But spruce cone seeds are their favorite.

These squirrels do not just use the seeds from the cones. They also make nests in underground burrows using cone scraps. Red squirrels prefer tree-hollow dens or leaf nests about 40 feet up in the trees.

WHERE TO FIND IT

Red squirrels live in any kind of forest with pine trees, hardwood trees, or both. Often, they live near buildings.

They can be found in the Rocky Mountain states, from Canada to Arizona and New Mexico. They also live in the Midwest, from Iowa to Ohio. And in the East, from Maine south to Georgia.

DOUGLAS' SQUIRREL

WHAT IT EATS

The Douglas' squirrel likes pine cone seeds best. It climbs high and cuts down green pine cones. Those it does not eat, it stores in damp places under logs, stumps or rocks, where they keep for 2 or 3 years. It also eats nuts and berries. Sometimes the Douglas' wedges mushrooms in tree forks to dry, then eats them later.

WHAT IT LOOKS LIKE

The Douglas' is one of the smallest tree squirrels, only 10 to 14 inches long. It weighs just over 1/2 pound. And this little squirrel is the most rowdy of all squirrels. It may drop 5-pound pine cones from 150 feet high onto a camper's tent!

The Douglas' squirrel is dark red-brown on its back, with rusty yellow undersides. Along each side, a black line separates its brown back from its yellowish belly. In winter, it grows small tufts of black hair on its ears. Its tail has a whitish fringe.

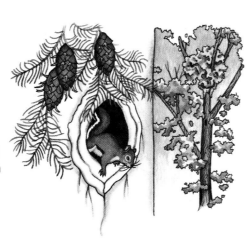

WHERE TO FIND IT

This squirrel likes to nest in a fir tree hole. But it also builds twig-and-leaf nests high up in pine trees. The nest looks like a big ball of leaves.

Douglas' squirrels can be found in the northwestern United States in Washington, Oregon, and south into California in tall pines and spruces.

ABERT'S SQUIRREL

WHAT IT LOOKS LIKE

The Abert's is the best-dressed squirrel in the West. It looks like it is wearing a white vest and white, fluffy tails. The long, black hairs on its head in winter look like a "top hat."

An Abert's squirrel weighs about 2 pounds, and is around 20 inches long. Its back is reddish-brown, and its sides are gray. Its tail is gray-white on top, with white underneath.

On the ground, Abert's squirrels carry their tails in a question-mark curve. They look clumsy when they walk, but they can run in smooth leaps along the ground.

WHAT IT EATS

Abert's squirrels eat acorns, seeds, berries and fungus. But its main food is the inner bark of ponderosa pine trees. It also eats spikenard roots and mistletoe.

INTERESTING FACTS

Abert's squirrels are very patient. Hiding from predators, they can lie still without twitching a tail hair for up to 2 hours.

WHERE TO FIND IT

The ponderosa pine is home for the Abert's. It builds a leaf nest on a twiggy platform, as wide as 3 feet. The nest's sturdy walls keep out winter's chill.

Abert's squirrels live in the southern Rocky Mountains. They can be found in Colorado and Utah, New Mexico, and around the Grand Canyon of Arizona.

KAIBAB SQUIRREL

At first glance, because of its black-and-white coloring, a Kaibab is often mistaken for a skunk. But kaibabs walk along gracefully, while skunks move with an awkward waddle.

WHAT IT LOOKS LIKE

Kaibabs are tassel-eared squirrels. Tufts of hair up to 2 inches long grow on their ears in the winter and stay until June, then they are shed. Kaibabs are about 19 to 21 inches long, and weigh 1 1/2 to 2 pounds. This squirrel is dark brown-gray all over, except for its snow-white tail.

Kaibab squirrels are very shy, and not nearly as noisy as other squirrels. You might walk under a tree where a Kaibab is without knowing it, because it keeps quiet.

WHAT IT EATS

Kaibabs feed on the soft inner bark of the ponderosa pines where they live. They eat mushrooms that grow under the needles covering the forest floor. They open apples just to get the seeds. Acorns, berries and roots are also Kaibab food.

WHERE TO FIND IT

Kaibab squirrels live only on a mountaintop across the Grand Canyon from Abert's squirrels. The plateau they live on towers 9,000 feet high. They live in the forests up there and cannot get down.

Kaibab squirrels build twig-and-needle nests, sometimes 89 feet up in the fork of a pine tree.

FLYING SQUIRREL

WHAT IT LOOKS LIKE

The flying squirrel only comes out after dark. This "flyer" does not really fly. It spreads the folds of skin that connect its front and back legs and glides like a kite on the wind in perfect silence.

Flying squirrels always land lower than where they take off. So they must climb up again for the next glide. Doing this, they can still go farther and faster than a person can keep up on the ground.

The northern flying squirrel is about 1 foot long. Its fur is a rich tan to cinnamon-brown, with dull white undersides. The southern flying squirrel is only 8 to 10 inches long. It is silky gray-brown, and creamy-white underneath.

WHAT IT EATS

Flying squirrels fuel their flight by eating bugs, acorns, hickory nuts, cherries and sunflower seeds. They also eat sugar maple blossoms, pine berries, lichens and bark. One flying squirrel family can eat a quart of June bugs in one meal.

WHERE TO FIND IT

Either the northern or southern flying squirrel can be found in every state except Colorado, New Mexico and Arizona. They make their dens in hollow trees, often in old woodpecker nests. They also build leaf nests.

Flying squirrels also have been known to move into bird houses, garages, attics, chimneys and mailboxes.

25

ROCK SQUIRREL

WHAT IT LOOKS LIKE

Rock squirrels are twice as long and twice as heavy as most ground squirrels. They grow up to 21 inches long and are as heavy as 2 pounds.

A rock squirrel does climb trees, but mostly it climbs around rocks. Its peppered, gray-brown fur helps it hide among those rocks. Its tail is brown and white. Its ears are smaller than most tree squirrels' ears.

WHAT IT EATS

Rock squirrels love to eat piñon nuts and acorns. They gobble up fig, cactus and wild gourd seeds, juniper berries, apricots and peaches. Rock squirrels eat seeds out of watermelons, and dig up newly planted corn. They also pounce on grasshoppers and earthworms.

INTERESTING FACTS

Rock squirrels got their name because they love to sit and sunbathe on the rocks.

WHERE TO FIND IT

A rock squirrel tries to make the door to its burrow between rocks so the door cannot be chewed bigger by enemies. Because of this, the squirrel does not have to hide its door like other ground squirrels do. It just leaves its dug-out dirt piled by the door. Sometimes the pile of dirt is enough to fill a barrel!

Rock squirrels can be found in the desert Southwest. They live from Oklahoma west to Nevada and California, and from Utah and Colorado south to Arizona, New Mexico and Texas.

THIRTEEN-LINED GROUND SQUIRREL

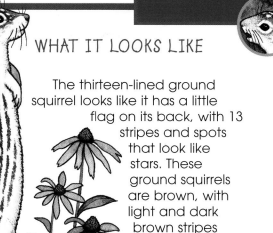

WHAT IT LOOKS LIKE

The thirteen-lined ground squirrel looks like it has a little flag on its back, with 13 stripes and spots that look like stars. These ground squirrels are brown, with light and dark brown stripes and light brown spots and undersides.

A thirteen-lined ground squirrel grows about 11 inches long. It weighs about 1/2 pound. When it comes out of hibernation in April, it weighs half as much as it did in October.

WHERE TO FIND IT

Thirteen-lined ground squirrels can be found all over the middle of the United States from Canada to Texas, and Utah to Ohio.

INTERESTING FACTS

The thirteen-lined ground squirrel really has about 23 stripes. But some are just broken lines that look like lines of spots.

WHAT IT EATS

The thirteen-lined eats a wide variety of foods. Oats, wheat, beans, sunflower seeds, cottonseed, goosefoot, knotweed and buffalo-bur are part of its diet. It also eats crickets, ants, beetles, wireworms, June bug grubs and butterflies. It likes frogs and even mice too. Grasshoppers are their favorite snack.

Look for it on golf courses and along roadsides, in most any mowed grass. It is often seen standing by its burrow, straight as a tent stake, front paws tight against its chest. If it senses danger, it will dive underground, then poke its nose out and make a bird-like noise.

GOLDEN-MANTLED GROUND SQUIRREL

WHAT IT LOOKS LIKE

This ground squirrel looks like a chipmunk, but it is bigger. One sure way to recognize it is by the reddish-brown "golden cape" around its head and shoulders. Also, it does not have face stripes like a chipmunk. The golden has a white stripe on each side between two black stripes, and yellowish-white tummy. Gray-brown fur covers its back and lower sides.

Above and below the eyes of a golden-mantled ground squirrel is a bright white crescent. Together, the crescents look like a ring around each eye.

The golden-mantled grows from 9 to 12 inches long. It is 3 times as heavy as most chipmunks. Most ground squirrels have tiny ears, but this one has large, rounded ears.

WHAT IT EATS

Fruits, seeds and nuts are this ground squirrel's main foods. A few of their favorite fruits are strawberries, cherries, Oregon grapes and thimbleberries. They also eat the seeds of yellow pine, Douglas fir and silver pine trees.

WHERE TO FIND IT

This ground squirrel is found on pine mountain slopes, among rocks and fallen trees. They are in every state west of a line down through Montana, Wyoming, Colorado and New Mexico.

HANG A SQUIRREL NUT-BALL

Squirrels love all kinds of nuts. If you hang up a squirrel nut-ball, you will have fun watching them try to catch it—and maybe even swing from it! Don't worry if they pull it down—that's fun too!

WHAT YOU NEED

▼

- All the nuts you can find. It is better if they are in the shell. But shelled peanuts—and even kernels of corn—will also work.
- peanut butter
- wax paper
- a piece of thin wire about 12 inches long
- a piece of string or cord 5 feet long

WHAT TO DO

▼

1 Roll the nuts in a thin coat of peanut butter. Place each nut on the wax paper.

2 Make little balls of nuts by sticking smaller nuts together. Bigger nuts do not need to be stuck to others just yet.

3 When you have about ten big nut clusters, stick them all together in one big ball. The nut-ball should be about 6 inches across.

4 Set the ball aside on the wax paper for a couple days to let it harden.

5 Push the wire through the center of the nut-ball, so half is sticking out on each side. Twist the ends of the wire together.

6 Tie one end of the string to the wire loop.

7 Tie the other end of the string to the branch of a tree. Make sure the ball hangs so it is not resting against the tree trunk, but will swing in all directions.

CHIPMUNKS

It may surprise you that chipmunks are also ground squirrels, a special kind. It is difficult even for animal experts to tell the many kinds of chipmunks apart. Some look as alike as twins. The best way to tell what kind of chipmunk you see is by where you are, because almost every kind of chipmunk lives in its own separate area.

All chipmunks have stripes on their faces. They are lighter than other ground squirrels. They weigh from about 1 ounce to 5 ounces. If a chipmunk is said to be brown-gray, it is because that kind will be browner in summer, grayer in winter. In dry deserts, chipmunk colors will be lighter, and stripes less clear. In sunnier, open forests, colors will be brighter, and stripes easier to see.

Chipmunks have pouches opening in the back corners of their mouths. The pouches run down along both sides of their necks. They carry their food in these pouches.

Chipmunks hibernate in burrows in winter, but not like bears. They deep-sleep, but wake up every few days to eat.

The sound chipmunks make is usually a "chip, chip," from which their name comes. But it may sound like "chuck" or "chock."

Chipmunks scamper and scurry around in the daytime. They are fun to watch as they look for nuts and other goodies!

EASTERN CHIPMUNK

The eastern chipmunk's heart beats nearly ten times as fast as yours—around 700 beats per minute.

WHAT IT EATS

The eastern always seems to be looking for food. It stores most of it in its burrow for its long winter sleep.

A list of every food the eastern eats and stores would fill this whole page. It likes all kinds of seeds, nuts, berries and fruits. They love flowers like the star flower, bugs like millipedes and ants, and frogs.

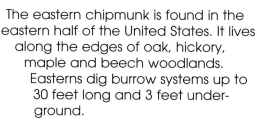

WHAT IT LOOKS LIKE

The eastern chipmunk has a wide, dark center stripe down its back. On each side it has a white stripe between 2 black stripes. That equals 7 stripes in all on its back and sides. The side stripes run from its neck to its behind, which is reddish. This chipmunk is 8 to 12 inches long. It weighs 2 to 4 ounces.

Eastern chipmunks usually run with their tails straight out behind them, unlike some other chipmunks that run with their tails pointing straight up.

To unload acorns from their cheek pouches, eastern chipmunks squeeze their cheeks with their front paws and out pop the acorns!

WHERE TO FIND IT

The eastern chipmunk is found in the eastern half of the United States. It lives along the edges of oak, hickory, maple and beech woodlands. Easterns dig burrow systems up to 30 feet long and 3 feet underground.

TOWNSEND'S CHIPMUNK

Townsend's chipmunks that live near the ocean coast are darker colored than those that live farther inland. The moist air near water makes their fur darker.

WHAT IT LOOKS LIKE

Townsend's chipmunks are the darkest-colored of all chipmunks. They are dark red-brown, and even their light stripes are not very white. The edges of its stripes are not as clear as most chipmunks' and its dark stripes are brown rather than crisp black. It has 9 stripes in all.

They grow between 9 and 11 inches long and can weigh up to 3 ounces. You can tell a Townsend's chipmunk by the bright red fur on the underside of its tail.

WHAT IT EATS

The Townsend's eats nuts, seeds and berries. In summer, it gulps down many kinds of berries. By fall, it switches to acorns, maple seeds and pine cone seeds. A special treat for a Townsend's is hazelnuts.

WHERE TO FIND IT

Townsend's chipmunks do not always live on the ground. This big chipmunk's nest of sedge and lichen is usually under a tree stump, but is sometimes in a tree.

A Townsend's chipmunk's burrow is usually under yellow pine, redwood, hemlock or fir trees. They live in Washington and Oregon, west of the Cascade Mountains. They are in northern California, too, along the Pacific Ocean, and down into the Sierra Mountains into Nevada.

MERRIAM'S CHIPMUNK

WHAT IT LOOKS LIKE

The stripes of the Merriam's chipmunk do not stand out as brightly as other chipmunks' stripes. Its sides are gray, and so are all its light stripes. The dark stripes are brown. The stripes on its head are 3 grays plus 2 browns. It has dull black spots at the eye corners, and a gray-white tummy.

The Merriam's chipmunk grows to be about 11 inches long. About half of that length is the tail. It has a longer tail than other chipmunks. This chipmunk can weigh about 2 to 4 ounces.

WHAT IT EATS

Merriam's chipmunks like to eat the small piñon pine nuts. They eat fruits like juniper berries, and seeds from the blue lupine. Merriam's chipmunks also munch the flowers and leaves of shrubs such as the manzanita.

WHERE TO FIND IT

It makes a nest about the size and shape of a coconut in its burrow. The burrow is dug under the stump of a ponderosa, yellow or digger pine tree. This chipmunk can be found in the brush and woodlands of the southwest quarter of California, from San Francisco to Mexico.

CLIFF CHIPMUNK

WHAT IT LOOKS LIKE

This chipmunk is a cliff-climber, and uses its tail to steer itself. If it falls, it twirls its tail like a tiny helicopter and lands softly.

The cliff chipmunk has a gray coat, with touches of brown, and gray-white patches behind its ears. Its bright white face stripes sometimes stand out. The black stripe down the middle of its back is its boldest dark stripe, but it is not always clear. The stripes on its sides are often blurry, too. One tell-tale sign of a cliff chipmunk is the rust-red beneath its tail.

Cliff chipmunks are medium-sized chipmunks, between 8 and 11 inches long. They weigh 2 to 3 ounces.

WHAT IT EATS

Cliff chipmunks feast on piñon nuts and juniper berries. They also eat grass seeds, insects and bird eggs. In dry times, they eat juicy cactus fruit.

WHERE TO FIND IT

Cliff chipmunks live in rocky mountains and canyons in Oregon, Idaho, Wyoming, Nevada, Utah, Colorado, Arizona and New Mexico. You can see them in Grand Canyon and Zion national parks.

Their burrows may be underground, or they may use cracks in the cliffside with nests of dried grass.

INTERESTING FACTS

A cliff chipmunk sways its tail back and forth to send an alarm, unlike the flicking, up-and-down tail motions that most chipmunks use.

UINTA CHIPMUNK

WHAT IT EATS

The Uinta eats mostly nuts, seeds and fruits. Piñon pine nuts, yellow-pine seeds and juniper berries are its usual meals.

WHAT IT LOOKS LIKE

Uinta chipmunks live where winter is cold, so they hibernate longer than most western chipmunks. To carry in enough food for winter, it uses its inner chipmunk cheeks like shopping carts.

A Uinta chipmunk is gray on the top of its head and behind its neck. It has two black spots at its eye corners that look almost like a stripe. Uintas have gray hips and reddish sides. The lowest side stripe is pure white and the dark stripes are blackish.

Their tails are grayish-black, and their tummies are creamy-white. Uintas grow to be 8 or 9 inches long and can be as heavy as 2 to 3 ounces.

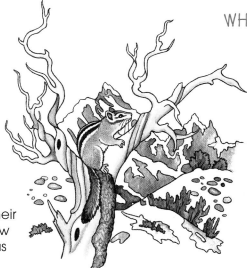

WHERE TO FIND IT

Uintas live high in mountain spots in parts of Wyoming, Colorado, Utah, Nevada, Idaho and Montana. A few can also be found in Arizona and California.

LODGEPOLE CHIPMUNK

INTERESTING FACTS

This chipmunk got its name because it is usually found around lodgepole pine trees.

WHAT IT LOOKS LIKE

The top of a lodgepole's head and neck are bright brown in summer and its sides are rust-red. Its lowest light side stripe is very white, and is wider than the other light stripes. Its dark and light stripes stand out like a zebra's.

A lodgepole is about as long and heavy as an ear of corn-on-the-cob. It is about 7 to 9 inches long.

WHAT IT EATS

Manzanita bushes make a two-course meal for lodgepoles, because they eat both the flowers and the berries. They also eat small nuts like piñons and fungus. Caterpillars are eaten, too, but usually only when there is not much other food.

WHERE TO FIND IT

Look for this climbing chipmunk around and in lodgepole pines, where those straight-trunk trees grow close together. Often, manzanita bushes will be near a lodgepole's burrow.

The lodgepole chipmunk is found in central California and in Nevada at the bend in its western border.

Lodgepole chipmunks like to live on the west sides of mountains where the ground is wetter.

YELLOW-PINE CHIPMUNK

One yellow-pine chipmunk's burrow had 67,970 pieces of food in it, including 15 kinds of seeds and part of a bumblebee.

WHAT IT EATS

The yellow-pine's handy "hands" easily pick the seeds out of strawberries and gooseberries. It eats mostly seeds, plus fruits, buds and fungi like mushrooms.

Yellow-pine chipmunks are not such eager nut-eaters as other chipmunks. These chipmunks love seeds, and it does not matter if they are ripe or still green. They eat the seeds of knotweed, yarrow, larch, thistle, huckleberry and yellow-pine trees.

WHAT IT LOOKS LIKE

The lightest and brightest chipmunk of all is the yellow-pine chipmunk. Some even say its brown-red sides are cinnamon-pink. The yellow-pine has stripes that stand out clearly on its face and body as well.

This chipmunk grows no longer than 10 inches, and weighs up to 2 1/2 ounces. A yellow-pine is yellow-white on its underparts, and the underneath of its tail is a brown-yellow.

WHERE TO FIND IT

Yellow-pines live east of the Cascade Mountains in Washington and Oregon, and along the eastern slope of the Sierra Nevada Mountains in California, over into Nevada. These bright chipmunks add color to the Rocky Mountains in Idaho, Montana, Wyoming and Utah.

LEAST CHIPMUNK

WHAT IT LOOKS LIKE

As its name says, the least chipmunk is little. A newborn least is only as big as a thimble. Most leasts are under 9 inches long. They always run with their tails up.

The colors of a least chipmunk's sides vary from orange-brown to dark gray, and it comes in more different colors than any other chipmunk. Unlike other chipmunks, the least's middle black back stripe runs from head to tail. Their tummies are gray-white.

WHAT IT EATS

Least chipmunks love berries, but they leave the pulp and take only the seeds. Blueberries, raspberries, strawberries and thimbleberries are their favorites. In spring, they eat grasshoppers, beetles and caterpillars.

WHERE TO FIND IT

Least chipmunks are excellent climbers, and may even nest in a tree, or just sun themselves on a branch.

Least chipmunks are found in more places than any other western chipmunk. They burrow into sagebrush desert and high mountains from North Dakota south to New Mexico, west through Arizona to California, and north to Washington. They also scamper through pine forests in Michigan, Wisconsin and Minnesota.

INTERESTING FACTS

In summer, least chipmunks may live in abandoned woodpecker holes or sleep in a tree nest of leaves.

MAKE A CHIPMUNK SWIMMING POOL

Some animals swim regularly, even some rabbits. Most all animals can swim, if they have to. And if you set up a swimming pool for the chipmunks, they will want to swim. Just make sure the pool is not deep.

WHAT YOU NEED

▼

- a shallow, flat-bottomed bowl, basin or tub (at least 18 inches across and no deeper than 4 inches)

- a garden hoe or shovel

- water from a hose or bucket

- a peanut in the shell, or another type of nut that floats

WHAT TO DO

▼

1 Pick a spot on the ground where you want to set the swimming pool. Put it near where you have seen chipmunks.

2 Using the hoe or edge of the shovel, scrape the ground a little so that the bowl will not wobble.

3 Put about 2 or 3 inches of water in the bowl.

4 Let it stay there for a day or two, so that the chipmunks get used to it. They might even try to drink from it.

5 After a day or so, float a peanut in the bowl. Then go away and watch from a distance.

The chipmunks will want the peanut, and even swim for it. Some chipmunks will even take a "bath" to get the peanut. After you have floated a few, and the chipmunks have gone swimming for them, you might even hear them scolding you if you forget to fill the pool, or forget to put peanuts in it!

For More Information

MORE BOOKS TO READ

Discovering Rabbits and Hares. Keith Porter (Watts)
Harper & Row's Complete Field Guide to North American Wildlife.
    Henry Hill Collins, Jr. (Harper & Row)
Mammals. Wonderful World of Animals series. Beatrice MacLeod (Gareth Stevens)
Rabbits and Hares. Animal Families series. Annette Barkhausen/Franz Geiser (Gareth Stevens)
Rabbits and Other Small Mammals. Charles Osborne (Time-Life)
World Guide to Mammals. Nicole Duplaix and Noel Simon (Crown Publishers)

VIDEOS

Chipmunks. (Phoenix/BFA)
The Rabbit. (Barr Media)

WEB SITES

www.ics.uci.edu/`pazzani/4H/Rabbits.html
library.advanced.org/11922/mammals/squirrel.htm

Some web sites stay current longer than others. For further web sites, use your search engines to locate the following topics: *chipmunks, hares, jackrabbits, rabbits,* and *squirrels.*

INDEX